Iguanas

by Grace Hansen

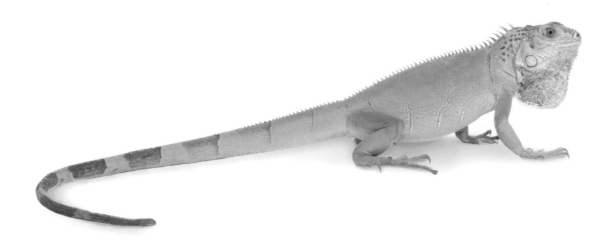

ABDO
REPTILES
Kids

www.abdopublishing.com

Published by Abdo Kids, a division of ABDO, P.O. Box 398166, Minneapolis, Minnesota 55439.

Copyright © 2015 by Abdo Consulting Group, Inc. International copyrights reserved in all countries. No part of this book may be reproduced in any form without written permission from the publisher.

Printed in the United States of America, North Mankato, Minnesota.

052014

092014

 THIS BOOK CONTAINS RECYCLED MATERIALS

Photo Credits: Getty Images, Glow Images, Shutterstock, Thinkstock

Production Contributors: Teddy Borth, Jennie Forsberg, Grace Hansen

Design Contributors: Candice Keimig, Laura Rask, Dorothy Toth

Library of Congress Control Number: 2013952327

Cataloging-in-Publication Data

Hansen, Grace.

Iguanas / Grace Hansen.

p. cm. -- (Reptiles)

ISBN 978-1-62970-059-5 (lib. bdg.)

Includes bibliographical references and index.

1. Iguanas--Juvenile literature.   I. Title.

597.95--dc23

2013952327

Table of Contents

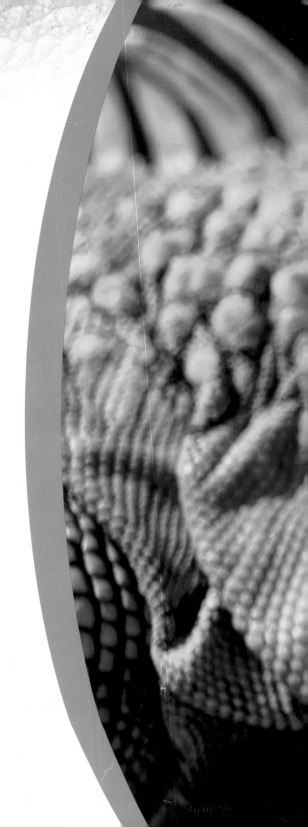

Iguanas

Iguanas are reptiles.

All reptiles have **scales**

and are **cold-blooded**.

4

5

Iguanas live in Central
and South America.

They also live in Mexico
and the Caribbean Islands.

Many iguanas live in rainforests. They live high up in the trees.

Some iguanas are brightly colored. Others are **dull** in color.

An iguana has a long tail.

Its tail helps it to **balance**.

Its tail helps it to swim too.

Food

Iguanas eat fruit and plants. Young iguanas eat insects and spiders too.

14

Baby Iguanas

Iguanas rarely leave the trees. Females will climb down to lay their eggs.

16

The female digs a **burrow**.
She lays her eggs in the
burrow. Then she climbs
back into her tree.

A baby iguana is on its own after **hatching**. It finds a branch to call its home.

More Facts

- Iguanas like to live near water. They are very good swimmers.

- Sometimes, an iguana will sit on a branch above water. If it feels scared, it can jump into the water and swim to safety.

- Some think that iguanas communicate with each other by moving their eyes very quickly.

Glossary

burrow – an animal's underground home.

cold-blooded – reptiles and fishes whose blood temperature changes with the outside temperature.

dull – not bright, little color.

hatch – to be born from an egg.

rainforest – a tropical forest with heavy rainfall. Filled with tall trees and many plants.

scales – flat plates that form the outer covering of reptiles.

Index

abdokids.com

Use this code to log on to abdokids.com and access crafts, games, videos and more!

Abdo Kids Code:
RIK0595